BEYOND SLEEP

PART I

OSEMER

ISBN Softcover 978-1-950596-78-2

Printed in the United States of America.

To order additional copies of this book, contact:
Bookwhip
1-855-339-3589
www.bookwhip.com

CHAPTER 1

My father used to sit under the summer sun in the small garden in front of our house, reading the news of the day. Then came the cold, cold winter, which made him tremble, especially in our old dilapidated home. It was just the two of us living there. My mother had died giving birth to me. I missed my mother's voice, even though I'd never heard it.

My father showed me pictures of her. "My son," he said, "she loved you while she bore you. And she thought about what you would become when you grew up. Before she gave birth to you, she asked me to name you Osemer."

If death made me hear my mother's voice, even for a moment, I wanted it today. But my mother was gone from this life, and I had only my father—my father, sick and on his deathbed. I cried so hard, I thought the walls of the house would fall upon me.

I said to my father, "Do not go. Stay with me. I do not know what to do if you leave."

My father encouraged me, saying, "Do not cry, Osemer. Stay strong. You will be the man of the house after me."

I thought, *A man in a lonely house. What is the benefit? Do I talk to the walls or talk to the doors?*

My father told me, "Do not be afraid, Osemer. We will all go someday. You are 15 years old now. You can go to school and do anything on your own. Do not mess with bad friends, Osemer. Do not ever believe that your mother did not love you. My son, she loved you more than herself. She even bought you clothes while you were in her stomach."

"My father, do you have more pictures of my mother I can keep with me?"

"No, Osemer. I already gave you all the pictures. Go now to the vault and bring me what's inside it."

I was surprised at the request. I went to the vault and extracted a cloth tied tightly. I took it to my father unopened.

Before he opened the cloth, he told me, "Osemer, listen to what I'm going to say. Don't open it, or you will be killed."

I was terrified. I didn't know what to say or ask my father. *Killed? Why?* I was so overwhelmed, I blacked out a little bit. When I awoke early in the morning and saw my father's dead body, I cried bitterly until my eyes had no more tears. Then I saw the cloth in his hand.

I ran out of the house, looking for help. I saw a man at the corner just about to enter his house. I cried out, "Please call the police!"

He left his breakfast at his door and hurried to me. As we entered my house, he tried to call 911. The moment he saw my father's body, he asked, "Son, what's your name?"

"Osemer."

"Your father wants you to be strong and know that his son can do anything he wants. He is a man. He does everything in life, and he is sure of it."

I could barely see because of my tears. I knew my father was gone, and I was now alone.

When the police came, I hurried to my father's body, took the cloth, and hid it in my pocket. *This cloth may be my only memory of my father*, I thought, crying. I said, "Dad, I'll do whatever you want. I'll stay strong."

My aunt Susan came over with her 9-year-old daughter, Julia; her son, Matthew; and her husband, Logan. She calmed me, as did her husband. He was a good man who treated me like one of his sons. Susan, Logan, and their children stayed with me for almost two years. The house was large, though old and worn.

One day, I was playing with Matthew when my aunt called us: "Matthew, Osemer, come in." After a long time of playing in the garden, we all came to lunch like one family. My aunt said, "Listen to me, Osemer. You're one of this family. If you want something, tell me or Uncle Logan. And don't be afraid of anyone."

I replied, "OK."

After lunch, Matthew and I went out a little bit and then to the park. We also played in the basement. We played, and I put the cloth back in its place in the vault.

CHAPTER 2

Finally, the time came for my aunt and uncle and cousins to return to their home. Aunt Susan prepared her things and those of her children and Logan. To me, she said, "All right, Osemer, we have to go now. I know you can take care of yourself."

"OK, Auntie," I said. "I hope you have a safe trip." We said goodbye, and they left.

As night went on, I thought, *This is the first day without my aunt and her family. It is my first day at home alone.*

I went to bed and fell asleep very fast. But suddenly, a sound woke me. *What is that?* I wondered.

I looked around the house, and the sound seemed to be coming from the vault with the cloth. There was also a sound coming from under the vault.

I took out the cloth and opened it. Inside was a key that shone so brightly. Oh, my God, how beautiful it was! But what was this this key? And for which door? I didn't know anything.

I heard voices all over the house, especially from the basement. I was so scared. *Who are they?* I wondered. I heard the voices over and over again. What made me afraid was that the voices were getting louder and louder. I told myself, *What's happening here is impossible. This is just a bad dream or a nightmare or my imagination.* So I went back to sleep.

When I woke up the next morning, I went out for a little bit to my friend Thomas's house. We lived in the same neighbourhood. He invited me to swim in their pool. Afterwards, we went to his room on the second floor of his house.

He asked, "Osemer, what's that in your pocket? Let me see it."

I told him, "This is a key that makes noises and makes things move in my house."

He asked me to let him try it for a little bit.

I said, "No. I don't want you getting hurt, Thomas."

He laughed. "Hey, Osemer, it's just a key."

"Listen, Thomas—you don't know what this key does! I will tell you."

"Who gave it to you, Osemer?" he interrupted.

"My father gave it to me before he died. OK, Thomas, I'm going to go before it gets dark."

As I went home, I again wondered, *What is this key for? Which door does it unlock?*

When I entered the house, I noticed the key start to light up. I went back out a little way, and the key became normal. I entered the house again, and it lit up again.

I sat playing with e-games and began hearing voices. I grabbed the key and started down the basement stairs. When I got to the bottom, I looked right but did not see anything. I looked left, and I didn't see anything there either. But I did notice a big old junk box way in the back of the basement.

I saw something black behind the box. It looked like a normal man, but that was impossible, because he sped to the wall and then suddenly disappeared.

I shuddered with fear, and I was mad that I couldn't prove what I saw. I ran to the door and hustled over to Thomas's house. I asked him, "Will you let me sleep in your room tonight?"

"Of course," he responded. "Why do you look so pale?"

I wanted to tell him what happened, but I knew he wouldn't believe me. So we sat down, and I remembered my father's words: "Be strong, and don't be afraid."

Thomas went to Cynthia, his mother, to ask her permission for me to spend the night. His father, George, was not there. George worked in shifts at a company a short distance from the city.

His mother agreed. We played until it was almost midnight. We grew tired, went to sleep, and awoke early in the morning.

Thomas's mother prepared breakfast for us. Then Thomas went with me to the cemetery. I put roses on my father's grave, but then I saw something odd at the end of the grave—a little black cloth. I took it with me, and I went back to my house. Thomas went home. I sat thinking about the mystery surrounding my father's death.

I grew tired of thinking. Then I remembered the thing I saw in the basement. I was sure that mysterious figure had something to do with my dad. I went looking throughout the house for any evidence, a cloth or something, but I didn't find anything.

Finally I went down to the basement, and I heard people talking in very low voices. I saw them as demons with long ears gathered in a circle talking like they were recording.

I heard someone say, "Osemer is 17 years old."

Another said, "His father died, and his mother died too."

Suddenly, the lights started turning off and on very fast. I didn't know what I was going to do. I went speeding to my dad's room, and I got in bed with the covers over my head. I kept saying, "It's not real, it's not real!" Sometimes I heard voices, and sometimes the lights turned off and on again.

What should I do? And how long would I keep saying this was a nightmare or a bad dream when I saw things happening? What was the story of these black demons? I was starting my journey with these creatures and this world, and I wanted to tell one of my friends, but I knew nobody would believe me. I would be alone in this way for the rest of my life.

When I finally went to bed and to sleep, I saw myself in a strange land. I couldn't believe what my eyes were seeing. I was sure that this was fiction or a dream, but I was also walking. The whole land was green, and I saw a river. So I went to this river and I drank a lot; I was thirsty. When I finished, I raised my head and was shocked to see an animal looking at me as if she wanted to kill me.

I woke up suddenly and I saw that all the windows and doors of the house were open. Then a strong wind hit the windows, closing all but one. At the last window, I saw a little piece of black cloth like the one that was on my father's grave. Who put it there?

I started thinking, *What does this have to do with the key?*

CHAPTER 3

During the night, while I was wandering around the house, I kept seeing that black imaginary man running fast. I was stunned. I went to my room and shut the door.

I thought to myself, *Why me? What's happening to me? Is this real?*

I lay down on my bed, thinking that if I slept, I'd be in that strange land again. When it happened, I saw the same black figure, and this time I followed him. I didn't know what he wanted. When he settled down behind some trees, I came to him. I couldn't see his face; it was covered.

"Who are you?" I asked.

He replied, "My name is William. I'm the one hired by your father to protect you, Osemer. I am a black fire demon."

"What does my father have to do with you?"

"Osemer," he said, "your father was wanted by the other demons. They wanted to kill him, but I had mercy on him, and I helped him. They wanted to kill your father, but when he came, I put him in a safe place so they wouldn't kill him."

I said, "But what did my father do to them that they wanted to kill him?"

He said, "Osemer, they want the key that your father gave you. And now, I'm afraid they'll have to kill you."

I asked, "Who are they?"

He said, "The demon masters. They have followers and animals under their power."

"How did my father get the key?" I asked.

"It was given to him by your grandfather, and in turn he gave it to you."

"I will go to them and fight them," I said, thinking to avenge my father.

"They are more than you in numbers and greater in strength," the demon responded. "You cannot get close to them. They have guards of the most powerful demons and more powerful animals. If you go to them, they will not leave you alive."

I said, "But when I wake up, they can approach me."

He said, "Yes, Osemer."

"And what is the story of this key?"

He said, "The demons have treasures and secrets. If you expose the secrets of the demons, you kill them. These secrets and treasures are hidden in underground tunnels and a safe that only you can open."

"I do not know what to do," I said. "I'm so confused."

"I know, Osemer. Some of my friends wish to eliminate these demons and want to accompany us on the trip, if we wish to leave and open the safe." He added, "I'm with you, Osemer—for wherever you want to go and whatever you want."

CHAPTER 4

When I woke up, I panicked and rushed to the window. The sky was red. The door of the house was closing and opening, and I heard the sound of glass crashing. I knew that the demons knew that I knew about the key.

I quickly searched for the key and found it lying on the bed. I asked myself, *Where is the one who came in the dream? Maybe he can come only in the dre*am.

I sat in front of the television as if I could not hear the crash of glass or the sound of screaming coming from outside. I did not give it my attention. But it was like there was a demon inside the television, showing a movie scene of the devil trying to kill me.

I saw myself in the television, and those who wanted to kill me were all around me. I heard a voice coming out of the television saying, "Kill him."

I said in the television, "No, do not kill me," but then I saw myself dead in the television. Sitting around me were two devils eating me, and William was there also. They tried to kill him, and he struggled to get out of their grip.

I saw myself dead in the television. One of the demons said, "Carry him to the morgue." It was if I was watching a documentary about myself.

I changed the channel, and then I saw myself sitting on the electric chair with demons running around me. I heard a voice almost shaking the place: "This is Osemer! This is Osemer! He is accused of not obeying the Great Satan, and his verdict is to kill Osemer with electric shocks."

Inside the television, I said, "Wait, wait, I will obey! I will obey!"

I changed the television to another channel. There I saw myself sitting on an execution platform. Standing in front of me was a man in a black cloak, and around him, animals and demons were screaming, "Kill him! Kill him!"

The man carried me to the podium. I was standing but as though I was tied to the podium The man took out a long knife and inserted it into my neck as I, still alive, shouted and screamed. Then he cut down until he reached my guts. My guts were pulled out, and animals and demons encouraged him and screamed.

My eyes became red and tired. I knew it was just a representation and acting from the demons to scare me.

I went and sat in the corner of my father's room for hours. I was in that corner afraid and trembling from what I saw in the TV. The voices came back up, and this was the cause of my fear. I hoped that the morning would come fast.

I wanted to go to the middle of the house to see the hour, but before I opened the door, I heard voices behind it whispering and talking. Then I heard the sound of the television, and I stayed in the room, shaking.

I did not sleep at all that night. I sat in the corner counting the minutes and the hours, with the sound of things hitting the door from outside the room. The question that was on my mind was, did my father suffer all this? Why did he not tell me of this psychological war?

I told myself there was nothing stronger than this that the demons could do to me. I put my head on the pillow of sadness, and between the bed of death and the cover of madness, I relaxed a little, somewhere between snooze and vigilance. Finally, the voices were gone. I looked from the window to the sky to see if it was normal. I went to the door, and I heard nothing. The television sound was gone.

I opened the door quietly so that no one would hear me, and I started looking from the side of the door. I saw nothing, and I said to myself, *If you are afraid now, they will know. I'm afraid of these voices, and they're increasing.* I didn't show them I was afraid, and they didn't do anything like the TV or the sky becoming red or glass crashing.

I went to the middle of the house, and sat in front of the big clock on the wall. I turned off the lights and sat down looking at the clock, like I was waiting for something. Then I heard *knock ... knock-knock ... knock.*

I looked at the clock. I didn't know what was happening to me. It was three in the morning, and the lights were off. I looked at my hand, and it was making weird movements, like the way a small baby moves his hands. It was as if someone was sitting in front of me, and I was welcoming him with these special movements.

I don't know how to describe this, but I did not feel anything. I just watched my body move, go to the kitchen, get a cooking kit, and then put it back. Looking, just looking. I couldn't control my hands or my legs.

Then I went to my dad's room, turned off the lights, and went to the corner. I lay down as if I was worshiping something in the corner of my father's room, but I did not see anything. Then I went to the toilet, locked myself in the bathroom, and lay in the corner of the room.

It was the worst night in my life. They did not leave off anything they could do to me. I could not do anything against them.

Finally, I came out of the toilet, and I was in control of myself again. I went to the basement and walked in, step by step.

I heard my father's voice saying, "Why did you do this?"

And a voice responded to him like the voice of a woman. I thought of my mother at this moment, and my legs could not carry my body. I fell on the stairs, and tears drained from my eyes.

I said to myself, *I want to see my mother, even if it is a lie.* I went towards the voice quickly, but I did not find anything.

Oh, my God, how sad I was. I did not pay attention to my father's voice due to the strength of missing my mother and missing her voice. Sadness overcame me, as if I saw the whole world against me. I thought of committing suicide.

But I changed my mind about suicide because that would mean I gave up to them. I would not give up, and I would not let go of what my father started. I went once again to my bed in my father's room, and I tried to sleep. I tossed and turned in my bed but would never surrender.

Sounds began to ascend, and I was in a bed that smelled of death. I embraced the image of my mother under the window, which was open. After this, I felt relaxed in the depths of my heart. I did not know why, but the morning breeze was in the room, and I knew that there was little time left for the dark cold night that had been like long years in my mind and heart. I felt good about this breeze that dried my tears.

Then I felt the intensity of fatigue and insomnia. How tired I was after this black night turned upside-down. I browsed my mother's pictures and imagined myself with her in every picture. I told myself what my mother would tell me if she saw me in this moment of madness.

CHAPTER 5

I fell into a deep sleep, and I returned to the strange land. I looked around for William. He stepped out from the bushes behind me and said, "You took a long time while you were awake."

I said, "Yes. They came despite my vigilance and did not let me sleep. I saw things and heard voices, and I could do nothing. How can I get rid of them?"

He said, "I told you, Osemer, we must go to the hiding places of their treasures and secrets and bring with us the key. Do you have the key, Osemer, or did you lose it?"

I said, "It's in my pocket."

"Well, OK, let's start," he said.

"But can they know where I am by this key?" I asked.

He replied, "I do not think so, Osemer. But if the key glows and shines, they will come to you in dreams." He added, "It is easy for them to get close to you while you are awake, because they are with you in the house."

I said, "I do not want to wake up. I want to stay with you in this land."

He said, "Well, Osemer, if you want to not wake up, you have to drink from a magical river behind that mountain."

I said, "Let's go!"

We started towards the mountain. We passed villages inhabited by animals. On my left side, I heard a cat say to a cow, "This is Osemer, who is wanted by the committee of witches and demons. There is a ransom for anyone who brings him in, alive or dead. It is important, this key. It is the end of devils."

Then William said to me, "I can go stealthily, and I can take on the shape of an animal, either a dog or a rat, and I can hear what they're saying."

I said to him, "After we get to that river, do whatever you want."

The mountain was so big. It would take time to climb. I sat to relax a little, and then I continued my journey until we reached the top of the mountain and I saw all around me villages and animals.

Then I looked in front of me saw a river, blue and clear.

"Oh my God, what a beauty!" I exclaimed.

William said to me, "Hey, Osemer, drink fast. We do not have a lot of time. The sun is starting to fall, and we do not know when the key will shine. That means they're going to come."

So I start drinking from the river, relishing every drop.

Again, William told me to hurry. "There's only little time," he said. "One of my friends lives nearby. We'll sleep in his house tonight. He's in one of these villages."

While we were running, there was a shaking in my pocket. When I took it out, the key was radiating light. William told me to put it in my pocket.

We came to a house, and William knocked on the door. When the door was opened by a wolf, I fainted.

CHAPTER 6

Five hours later, I woke up and heard talking by the fireplace. William was talking to the wolf, and they were drinking tea.

When William saw me, he came over and said, "Do not be afraid of Jeffrey. He has spent most of his life fighting devils. One day he was severely wounded, and I took him into my house and helped him. Now he will help us"

He added, "Jeffrey is nervous, Osemer. Do not say in front of him that he is an animal or anything. I'm the only one of the devils who is talking to him and his friend. He hates devils, and he is all alone. No one of the animals can approach him. He has his own way and does not like for anyone to look at him very long. He considers that person an enemy. This is his instinct."

Then he said, "Jeffrey, are you ready to start the journey?"

Jeffrey said, "Yes. We will go out in the morning. They are now searching and exploring the villages and farms. In the morning, you will not see them. Take what you can from the food and drinks. We will pass a long road of valleys, mountains, and rivers. It will be a difficult journey, my friends. Whatever I say to you, do it. I have passed these mountains and valleys more than once while I was hungry. Do not forget to hide the key well, Osemer."

We sat around the stove talking, the three of us. Jeffrey told us what happened to him with the demons.

"It was two years ago or more," he said. "I had two brothers, and I lost them. We were out hunting, and we were hungry. We passed more than a valley and more than a mountain, and we were very thirsty. We saw a hole filled with water, and we drank from it until we didn't feel thirsty, but we were still hungry.

"We had to finish our way in the dark, but we could barely see. We saw what looked like a good prey at a not very far distance, but my older brother said, 'Do not go. I think it is a hunting trap in the mountains. The demons hunt in the mountains. If they are looking for someone or something, it is better for us to go away.'

"Then my younger brother said, 'But there is no other prey! The night is long, and it could be our only food for three nights.'

"We all hesitated, but hunger was so strong that we ran to the prey at our greatest speed. As we approached the prey, we saw that it had a big black cover over it. Beneath the cover was a demon with two lions, and he released the lions on us. My brothers were very close to the lions, and I was away from them by a few feet. I tried to fight the two lions. One of them killed my brother within seconds and then came for me. I managed to escape and survive.

"Because of this incident, I have hated everyone around me, especially demons. They became my favourite food, and I hunted them everywhere. I would do anything to avenge my brothers."

The morning breeze blew through the room, and Jeffrey and William wanted to sleep a little bit and rest. This was their land; they slept and they woke up. I'd gone out of my land, and I didn't want that land.

CHAPTER 7

In the morning, I could see fog around the village. The key had stopped glowing and shining, so I walked outside a little bit. This was all new to me. Jeffrey's house was a little far away from the village, so I walked until I saw a gathering of animals. I don't know why I went to them.

I saw a cow and thought, *If this is a cow that gives milk to the villagers, I'm amazed at this village.* I laughed, and she gave me a glass of milk.

Then a big old dog came up to me and said, "Son, do you know who I am?"

I said, "No, no."

Then he said, "I'm the mayor of this village. Are you Osemer?"

I said, "Yes. There is no human being in this land but me. Anyone who sees me will know I am Osemer."

He said. "I get papers and calls from the witches and demons committee about whether you're in my village or not. If I tell them no, the one you are asking for is not in my village, and they find out you are in my village, you don't know what they're going to do to me! I'm just asking you, son, to take what you want from this village and get out before the discovery squad comes. If they see you here, they'll burn the whole village. I do not want this to happen."

I said, "OK, I'll go, but first I want some food and drink."

I went to the cow, and she gave me a box of milk. I went to the bakery. The owner was a small bear. I asked him to give me what he had, and he gave me some bread.

When I walked back to Jeffrey's house, I kept looking behind me. The mayor looked like he was waiting for me to leave the village. Maybe he would send for the devils. I rushed into the house, and I got my friends to wake up. I told them what happened to me in the village.

Jeffrey said, "I should kill that traitor mayor. He's dealing with them, didn't you know, Osemer?"

I said, "No, I didn't know, but I saw him giving me weird looks. We need to leave now."

Jeffrey closed his house and hid the key. We started our journey, the three of us, under clear skies and over green land.

After we had walked a long distance, Jeffrey said, "I have heard that this valley has a lot of trees and is dense and difficult to traverse. There are a lot of hyenas and snakes. We have to pass through this valley very quickly. It is almost not possible to see the end of it."

We started to go down into the valley. Jeffrey was in the front. He shouted to me, "Be careful until we are done with the slope."

There was a hyena behind the bushes, and Jeffrey howled at it and showed his fangs. The hyena hesitated to attack us or to leave us, and Jeffrey hit the ground. At the last moment, the hyena moved five steps back, like he regretted his decision.

The question on my mind then was, *Do the animals in this land have the same power as in my known land, or are they stronger here?* I wanted to ask Jeffrey this question, but I remembered William's words not to try to talk to him. Jeffrey was very nervous, and there was no chance of joking or talking. Since what happened to his brother, he only wanted to kill. William had advised me, "Do not be in front of Jeffrey when his fangs emerge or if he is angry."

We passed through the valley safely, and the night got darker. Jeffrey said, "If you want to sleep, let's go someplace safe." He took us to a place he knew—a small cave that could barely accommodate two.

Jeffrey said, "I'm going to keep one eye open and the other one asleep, and I'll protect you."

I knew that since I drank from that river, I would not be going back to my old land and my house, so I slept, woke up, ate, and drank in this land. I became one of the people of this land, and I found them more sympathetic and friendly to me than humans. I lived with animals who grieved and became sad with me and rejoiced to be happy with me, and this was better than living within the walls of that crushed house.

There was nothing left for me in my old land and my house. When I woke up there, I remembered my father's leaving or my mother's leaving. and while I walked around the walls, I saw old memories of me and my father. My old world took the dearest thing from me: my father. He was all I had.

A tear rolled down on my cheek from sadness for my old land. Then I slept, with my friends standing watch. We'd had a tiring, hard day.

CHAPTER 8

When we woke in the early morning, the fog was all around us, so we could not take in the beauty of the scene. We sat talking and looking at the fog. Then William went to search for some breakfast.

He came back with some eggs he found at the edge of the valley. He made a small fire with some wood crumbs and a little stick. As we ate our breakfast, the fog cleared, and it was the prettiest morning I'd seen since I came to this land.

We continued on our journey, through trees that were very dense and large. It was terrifying, and we were confused as we walked. Suddenly, Jeffrey told us to stop.

I said, "Jeffrey, there's no one here. See how quiet the trees are."

He said, "That's what worries me."

There was a weird smell, and I did have the feeling that there was someone around us. I wasn't mistaken.

Jeffrey said, "I am sure there are those who listen to us and spy on us," and then he cried out, "Run away! Run, come on, Osemer!"

I saw a demon in a cart with some fast animals coming on our left side. William was with me and protecting me. Jeffrey wouldn't let them catch me alive. I was tired, and I was getting close to falling. William was encouraging me: "Come on, Osemer. Hurry, Osemer."

We were running, trying to put a great distance between us and them. One of their fast animals, a cheetah, approached us. She put her mouth on my feet. When Jeffrey looked at her, she started to fight him.

Jeffrey attacked with his teeth and sharp fangs. I could see the cheetah's red eyes, and finally she made a noise indicating her surrender and escaped to her demon.

William and I looked at Jeffrey proudly. He had a limp due to an injury in his left foot. We hid behind one of those big trees. We looked out to see the cart speeding away, followed by swarms of animals. Then we started walking a little bit. Finally, we saw that behind the trees there were wonderful green plains.

Before we stepped out of the forest, William said, "Wait a minute. Look at what I see."

I said, "What in heaven's name?"

"It's the Eye of the Witches. Their guide who flies to the demons and tells them everything. She probably saw us somewhere in the village and told them it was better we didn't get out of the trees. They waited for us and hid behind the trees." He added, "Let's wait until these birds leave. We'll stay here to make sure they don't come back for us."

CHAPTER 9

We stayed until nightfall. I was afraid Jeffrey was going to lose a lot of blood, but he said, "Don't be afraid for me. I've been shot so many times."

William said, "There's a village in the middle of the plains. One of my old friends will heal you with herbs, Jeffrey."

We started out of the trees. Though we tried to carry Jeffrey, he refused. As we walked, William told us a lot about his friend Peterson, who we were going to see.

"We were born in this village together and grew up together," William explained. "We did everything together. Over time, however, my friend began to change. He did some weird things, and I doubted they were for the good. He waited for the villagers to sleep and then came out of the village to go to the cemetery. This happened every day until I finally said to him, 'Peterson. what are you doing every day at that cemetery?'

"And he told me, 'I don't go there. Maybe I was sleepwalking.'

"I believed him, but I still had my doubts. I decided to watch him one night. I saw Peterson go out of his house and head to the cemetery. I followed him, staying behind him wherever he went. I saw him dig up a grave.

"After that, he climbed the fence of a big farm and walked until he reached the poultry room. It seemed to be closed with a big lock. Peterson got out a big iron bar and hit the lock until it fell off. He entered the room, and I heard the sound of chickens screeching. He came out holding a black rooster. I hid behind a tree, but he walked right by and didn't even notice me. He started running like he was in a hurry. I stayed behind him until he reached his house, entered, and locked his door well. I watch through the window as, with the rooster well tied and bones from the graveyard beside him, Peterson went to his kitchen. But why?

"Then he brought out a big shiny knife. All the demons were around him doing magic work in the living room. Peterson and I had agreed that we would be against the evil that demons and witches do to these poor and weak animals. We came here and lived with these good animals; why should we work this magic on them when they did nothing to hurt us? We grew up on this thought. But when I saw Peterson killing that poor animal, and when I saw the blood, I knew this was someone else, not my friend.

"I ran off and sat behind a tree until morning. My heart was grieving. I woke up and went straight to Peterson's house. I saw a lot of carts all around. I wondered, *What do they want from Peterson? Where are they taking him?* Their heads were hidden under long black covers. I saw my friend get into a cart, and then I only saw the dust as their carts rode away.

"Once they left the village, the animals came out of their dens and holes. They looked at those distant carriages, relieved at the demons' departure. But I was sad that they had taken my friend. I wondered if he would come back, so I waited for him in the mountains. After night fell, I saw one carriage coming to the village as the villagers slept. I crept into the village to see if this carriage would stop in front of Peterson's house. It did, and he opened the door and stepped out. The cart went away fast, and I came running.

"'Peterson!' I cried. 'Where did you go? I missed you!'

"And he said to me, 'There was a little problem, but it's over now.'

"He told me to come in. I didn't want to make him angry and ask him about the magic he did, so I waited until we sat down.

"'What were you doing last night?' I asked.

"'I was asleep all night,' he told me.

"I said, 'Didn't you do magic last night? You went to the cemetery and dug bones out of a grave. I followed to keep an eye on you. You went to a farm and stole a black rooster. Why, Peterson? We said we were not going to do these things. They're evil and bad. We are against these things, and we have gone away from other villages just to get away from these evil things that bring the sparks of demons.

"He said, 'Yes, I was doing magic, I admit it. I'm just having a little fun.'

"That was the last thing that happened between me and him," said William. "We're close to his house now."

We came to Peterson's house and started knocking on the door. He opened it and said, "Welcome, welcome, my old friend!" He let us in and started preparing dinner. It was a turkey, the best that I ate on my trip.

Before the food was ready, William said, "Hey, Peterson, this is my friend Jeffrey, and this is Osemer."

Peterson said, "Osemer—I know him well!"

William said, "How do you know him, Peterson?"

He said, "In a way that does not leave walls and police stations and is required throughout the villages and even in the forest. When I go to trade rice and flour, I find wanted posters for Osemer. But don't be afraid. Here, you are safe, Osemer."

William said, "We came for you to help Jeffrey. His leg is injured. I saw you in the old days with medicines made of wild herbs. All the villagers came to see you."

He said, "Yes, yes, my friend. But I need some particular herbs; I don't have any, but I know where you and Osemer can get them. Osemer, you'll find a mountain behind this house. Climb up the mountain, walk fifty metres, and you will find bright green herbs. Bring me some. They are strong and will heal your friend."

Then he said, "William, go with the river. Stay with it until you end up in the lake. Then look at the plants on the edge of the lake. Gather a lot of them; they're good for all of us, even if we're not injured. Go before the night gets dark."

CHAPTER 10

William and I went on our way. The sun was about to say goodbye. My friend went with the river that was just in front of the village, and I went towards the mountain. It looked far away. I was running a little bit and then walking when I got tired. I was afraid of the valley I had to cross before I got to the mountain. I was afraid the animals in this valley would come out at night, so I started to run again. I wanted to pass the valley as soon as I could.

I remained in front of the mountain, but the mountain was great. My neck was almost broken trying to see the top of it. No wonder it contained healing herbs. As I climbed, I fell down on some rocks. I hoped I would not to fall from the big rocks.

I wanted to sit down a little bit, but Peterson had said I must bring this herb, and I didn't want to be late for Jeffrey. If something happened to him, I would never forgive myself. So I did not allow myself to get tired. Horrible voices were coming from the darkness, but it was important that I didn't give them my attention. I went about my business and found the herbs in the place Peterson had described.

On my way back out of the valley, I saw something I hadn't seen before. I saw a cave like a tunnel radiating a bright yellow light. I was hesitant, but I was also curious about this light. If I left, I wouldn't know what the story of this light was, and I'd keep thinking about it. But the cave was far away. I needed to get out of this valley. I was walking with the wall of the valley, and there were bushes. The valley was dense with greenery, almost to my chest.

Something rose up in front of my eyes from an abyss inside of the earth. There was a bush close to me, and I hid behind it. The creature didn't see me looking at him. He came out of the ground and went to the wall of the valley and then disappeared suddenly from the same place he came from. This creature wore a very long hats and had slender feet. I could just barely see his red eyes.

After I saw this, I ran and fell and ran again. I got lost, and then I saw light on my right, As I ran away, a figure passed on my left. I ran with him, and then he disappeared again. I knew that I would fall into their hands. They ran at the speed of the wind. Each of them carried a light in a box, and they ran straight at me like they were going to hit me. Then they disappeared, and I ran.

From the intensity of darkness, they came and ran by my side. I saw them holding their lights. I ran by a little tree and bumped into it. I ran and I closed my eyes and I put my head between my feet until they stopped running. They started casting sounds, and I was so scared.

Then I heard them digging. I didn't see them, but I heard the shovels, and I said to myself, *They must be digging a grave for me.* Then I looked in one hand and the other was closed, and I saw a light from there, and I saw in the light as if it was the village. I saw houses, and I ran as fast as I could before the light disappeared. Finally, I finally got to Peterson's house.

William asked me why I was late. "What have you been doing all this time?"

"They came to me," I told him.

William asked, "Who are *they*?"

I said, "They came from the valley. I don't know what they are. Their eyes are red, they wear very long hats, they come out of the ground, and they're fast. They must be demons."

William said, "Jeffrey has sweat too much and bled a lot of blood. If you see him, you will see the bones of his face. His face is too dry. Quickly, Peterson, take the herbs and help him."

Peterson said, "Hey, Osemer, your friend is badly hurt. Give me the herbs, quickly." He put some water to boil on the fire and hurried to get some equipment from the kitchen to prepare the herbs and grind them well. When he was finished with the herbs, he put them in a cup for Jeffrey to drink.

Jeffrey drank, and then he said with surprise, "Why, the injury in my foot has healed!" Peterson had tied it with a cloth to stop the bleeding.

Peterson said, "Yes, Jeffrey, but your body has been hurt because the wound has remained open for a long time."

Jeffrey continued drinking until the cup was empty, and then he returned to bed. Peterson said, "No one bother him. If he does not relax, the treatment will not take effect."

Then Peterson and William went to the fireplace and spoke. I lay down in the room in front of Jeffrey, and I began thinking about how the creatures disappeared, going straight to the wall. If that was their ability, why could William not do like them or Peterson? There was no explanation for what happened today unless they were dealing with magic. There were no demons so fast, and if there were, how did they disappear into the wall of the valley? My eyes weren't lying to me.

The question that worried me most was, what was that light in the cave? I wanted to go see it, but ... why did they come after me like they were protecting something in the cave? I got tired of thinking, and then Peterson interrupted me. He told me, "Come and have some tea."

I went to drink with them at the fireplace. Talking about this village, Peterson said, "All the animals in this village love me. Even the animals with the instinct for killing love me. If any of the villagers are sick, they come to me. I am the only one in this village who has medicines. It is not magic, and they don't need money. All my medicines are herbs, and I have treated half the village, so they love me."

He went on, "There was a time when they hated me, and I was alone. My house was in the desert. None of them talked to me, and now they're all talking to me, and they're thinking about making me the mayor of the village."

William said, "You deserve to be mayor. You tried and tried repeatedly to gain the love of this village, not with magic but with the medicines—with a noble and honourable goal. They should love you after you have treated them like this. I've known you since we were kids, Peterson, and so I want you to stay."

After that, we all slept. I felt so comfortable in that sleep.

CHAPTER 11

When I woke up in the morning, I looked for my friends. Peterson's bed was empty, so I went looking for him in the village, calling "Peterson! Peterson!"

I saw a large newly built structure, and I had the idea that this building was the office of the village mayor. Then I saw Peterson, and around him were half the villagers holding him on their shoulders and shouting, "Peterson, the mayor!"

He looked at me and came to where I was. "I woke up, Osemer, and they brought me here, and they told me, 'This is your position, and we want you to be our mayor,' and then they made me sign some paperwork."

"Well, congratulations, Peterson," I said. "Good for you."

I went back to Peterson's house to wake up William and check on Jeffrey. "William, William," I called out, "wake up. The sun is in the sky, and you're still asleep."

He got out of bed and stumbled towards the door.

"What is this, William?" I asked. "Do you devils sleep in a deep sleep, or are you a unique case? Go wash your face."

I went and took a cup of water to Jeffrey. "Wake up," I told him. "Come on. How are you doing?"

"Okay," Jeffrey said. "I'm starting to feel better. Open the window, Osemer. Let in the sunlight and the fresh air."

"Okay, just as you ordered," I said. "But Jeffrey, if you stay in bed lying down, you're going to get sick."

I wanted something from him, but I didn't want William to hear us.

Jeffrey said, "I'll walk out a little. I'll see you at dinner."

"Wait, Jeffrey," I said. "I want to go out with you."

We set out toward the village centre, and I said, "Look, Jeffrey, I want to tell you something, but I don't want you to tell anyone. Don't tell William."

He said, "I won't tell."

I began, "Yesterday, I went to the mountain to get you herbs, and I passed through a big valley. On the way back, I saw a shining light coming from a cave in the valley. I want you to go with me tonight without anyone following us, while Peterson and William sleep. I don't want them to get hurt. All right, Jeffrey?"

"Okay, Osemer," he said.

We talked and walked until the sun started disappearing, and then we came back home. We saw the whole village outside Peterson's house shouting—dogs, cats, cows, and birds of all kinds, all the villagers. When Peterson came out, they raised him high above their shoulders, shouting, "Peterson, Peterson, Peterson!"

Jeffrey said, "What is this?"

I told Jeffrey, "They made him the mayor of this village, given his herbal treatments and his great influence."

"Peterson, Peterson, Peterson—he is our mayor! Peterson, Peterson," they shouted. Finally, they put him down in front of the house. Two cats came to give to Peterson a stuffed turkey, which they put in the living room.

Peterson said, "Come on, everybody, let's eat. Come on."

William said, "If you become Mayor Peterson, command the village to bring you all sorts of food to your doorstep."

After we finished eating, we went to the park behind the house, and I started asking Peterson questions because of his knowledge of the village. "Peterson, there are demons' vaults, right?"

Peterson said, "Yes, everybody knows that."

Osemer then said, "Tell me, where are these vaults, Peterson?"

He replied, "No one knows where they are.

I said, "Okay, but do you know if they put the vaults in mountains or under their thrones? My dad, before he died, was telling me about hiding something either in a cave or in a river or underground. He said, 'You don't know where it is. You expect a dark and scary place with a safe. Osemer, it is well closed and only opens with a very special key.' I didn't understand, but I'd like to know. This is their power puzzle."

I looked at Jeffrey, and he looked at me. He winked at me. He was ready.

During my daytime walk with Jeffrey, I had gathered several leaves from a tree that brings sleepiness. I made tea with the leaves and gave it to William and Peterson. Jeffrey knew about it and did not drink any.

In about ten minutes, William and Peterson fell into sleep. They felt nothing.

I asked Jeffrey if he was ready. He said, "Come on."

I opened the front door very slowly so William and Peterson wouldn't wake up. Jeffrey came out with me, and we started on our way.

Jeffrey said, "Hey, Osemer."

I said, "What?"

He said, "If we go alone and we find them, maybe they're more than us, and we can't stop them."

I said, "Do you have an idea?"

He said, "Yes. I want to climb this nearby mountain just to get my friends to come with us."

"Okay, Jeffrey," I said.

We went up the big mountain. When we were standing at the summit, Jeffrey began howling and howling and continued howling until we heard another howl in response. Jeffrey said, "They're coming. Let's wait a little longer. They are quick and will come to us."

Soon I saw five wolves. "Oh, my God, how big they are!" I exclaimed

The wolves asked, "Do you want us to help, Jeffrey?"

"Yes," said Jeffrey. "I want you to help me with something in this valley."

They all said, "We are in the service of our own people."

CHAPTER 12

We started jogging to the valley. I saw the wolves giving each other motivational looks, saying to each other, "Don't be afraid. I've got your back." This was the type of animals they were and what they did. It made them stronger.

When we got to the valley, we started to go down one after another. When we were all in the dark fog of the valley, Jeffrey asked me, "Osemer, where's the cave?"

I said, "It's not far." We walked across the valley lengthwise, running as we approached the wall, and then we stopped at the entrance of the cave. We heard terrifying voices. We wait at the entrance for someone to come out of the cave, but no one did. So we entered. We do not know what the light was or how deep it was in the cave.

The closer we got to the light, the louder the screaming became. Finally, we stopped at a big underground yard. As we entered it, we saw a very big snake. When the snake saw the wolves, he hit the wall, and we saw dirt falling in a circle around this big snake. One of the wolves was in front of the snake, and the snake bit this wolf and would not let go. The other wolves attacked the snake, and they all bit the snake everywhere on his body, but he did not leave this wolf.

I went fast and grabbed the wolf's foot and tried to pull it out of the snake's mouth. It was only moments before the wolves' powerful jaw exposed the flesh of this snake from every side of his body. There was blood all over the cave, and finally the snake fell. It shook the whole cave.

The wolves gathered around the wolf who was bitten by the snake. Behind the snake, I found what I'd been expecting all along: the vault. The snake had been protecting it.

The wolves gathered around me. It was time to open the safe. From the moment I saw it, the key in my pocket—the magic key my father gave me—had started shaking. I pulled it out, and it was shaking in my hand, radiating beautiful colours. I looked into the vault, and oh my God, how beautiful it was. The wolves were telling me to open it up. So I inserted the key, and what happened was incredible and unbelievable.

The vault door opened, and I couldn't believe what my eyes were seeing. It was filled with gold and sparkling jewellery. I took as much as I could.

A black box placed behind the jewels attracted my attention, and I knew very well that the demons' secrets were hidden in it. I carried it with me and sped out of the cave. After we got out of the valley, I said to the wolves, "Thank you. You helped us a lot." And then they went back to their mountains.

Jeffrey stayed with me. He said, "What is this box, Osemer?"

"It's a big deal, I'm sure of it," I told him. "The next vault will cause panic and fear if we find it, and once I open it, they'll all know that their first safe has been opened and their secrets revealed."

We were very tired. We could barely hold our bodies up when we got to Peterson's door. We entered the house, and Jeffrey and I went straight to bed. I hope I didn't bother the village with my snoring.

CHAPTER 13

I slept all morning and didn't wake up until four in the afternoon. Peterson and William were gone. As I awoke, I remembered what had happened the night before and made sure the box was well hidden under my bed.

Jeffrey woke up also and came to sit next to me. I said, "Jeffrey, where are Peterson and William?"

He said, "They went to the mayor's office in the village."

We waited for them. They came in joyful and laughing; they didn't know anything about what had happened the night before.

I told them, "Fellas, I want to tell you something. Last night, Jeffrey and I went on a long trek, and we didn't go alone. Jeffrey summoned some of his mates."

I realized I had to do a little explaining first. "The other day, when I went through the valley to get the herbs, I saw a luminous cave. I never told you about it. But I agreed with Jeffrey that he and I were going to go to the cave to find out what that light was."

I continued, "It was guarded by a snake so big, it hurt Jeffrey's friend, and then we killed the snake and found behind it a vault. I put my key in it and it opened, and I wish you had seen what was in it. It was filled with beautiful jewellery.

"It's the beginning of the end for these evil devils," I went on. "It's part of their secrets and the beginning of their diseases. I won't stop looking for the vaults. I have the key in my purse. And now, my friends, I want to open the box. I'm going to get it now."

It was a very normal box, but it was black, and it had strange words engraved on it as an inscription. I brought it in and saw in their eyes those eager looks to know what was in the box.

Peterson said, "Open it. Open it quickly."

And then I opened it, and we all looked at it. All the colours came out of it in the form of strong bright lights, and we heard screaming on this earth—terrified screaming. I closed the box quickly. We were all a little scared.

"What is that scream?" I asked.

"It's the cry of their great master," said William. "They know about the vault."

I felt like I had planted a spear in their master's chest. The sky was starting to get dark, but not from the sun setting. It was as if they were flying and making heaven so black from their lot. They were out of the box.

We stayed inside the house until nightfall. The moon was shining, and the sounds were close by. We left the house and went to the park, and we saw the sky full of demons with fire, all of them flying in their long robes. It was a horrible sight.

We ran to the mountain in front of the village, and we started to climb up to the trees. We were hiding from one tree to another until we saw some of the demons come to the village and then fly over it and start throwing fire at the houses in the village, leaving the villagers terrified and screaming. Devils approached every fugitive from the village, examined each face, and then let each individual escape, as if they were looking for me. They knew I was the one who opened the vault, because no one had the key but me.

We climbed very fast to the top of the mountain where the trees were dense. We looked down and saw that the valley was full of them. They were returning to their master disappointed. We slept at the top of the mountain until the morning came and woke my friends.

Peterson said, "I pity the villagers who have been burned out of their houses. Now where are they going to go? They don't have anything except for those houses."

I said, "Don't be afraid. You'll see what's going to happen."

I wanted to go down to the village. When we got there, I saw villagers examining their burning homes. Some of them called out to us, so I asked Peterson to collect them.

When they had come together, I told them, "Listen. The reason for all these fires, and I hope you will forgive me, is to make this the most beautiful village. I want to give you my money and my jewellery. Stand in a row, and I will give you what you need to build better homes than the old ones."

I took out my purse and started giving them some of the gold bars and jewels I had taken from the vault. The first one came to me, and I asked, "How much gold do you need?"

"I want two bars," the villager responded.

"OK, take it. You're a beautiful cat."

When I had helped all the villagers, I said to my friends, "Now I will continue my journey forward. Who will complete it with me?"

There was a long moment of silence, and I could hardly bear it. Finally, Peterson said, "I can't go with you, Osemer. I want to stay here with the villagers. These are good creatures. I will not find a village better than this village. They love me here."

I said, "OK, buddy, it's your choice, but I won't let you go without giving you three gold bars—the last I have left. I want you to take these back to the village."

Then I looked at William. "Will you complete this journey with me?"

He said, "Yes, but not now. I want to stay with Peterson for a few days. I'll catch up with you."

I said, "OK, buddy, goodbye." The two of them went back to town.

I looked at Jeffrey, and he said, "There's nothing for me in this village. I'm going with you, Osemer.

I grabbed his shoulder. I knew that when wolves loved someone, they loved hard and with a big heart. We set out alone. The road was long. We came to the end of the trees and entered an arid, dry land. I was glad to be going on this quest with my friend.

CHAPTER 14

Jeffrey said, "Let's climb that mountain."

The mountain was on our right, so we started climbing and climbing. We came to a pure freshwater river, and we bathed it and sat down.

As we sat taking in this radiant river of sunlight, I said, "Jeffrey, I never saw my mother. I've only seen pictures of her."

I went on, "I was born alone without brothers or mother. I had only my father, who always encouraged me and strengthened me. He always said, 'Osemer is the man of the house.' I was always the sad boy in school who was silent all the time. Jeffrey, I love loneliness and sadness. I love everything that is sad or brings me grief, and I always say I wish I hadn't been born."

Jeffrey replied, "With wolves, our herd is one big family. Always the prey resists. When one of us dies, we grieve for him, but we don't stay sad all our lives. If you notice, Osemer, we wolves are never alone. Life may want to remove you and kill you, but you are naturally resisting and looking to secure for yourself a dream. And so life continues."

As we talked, we heard the same screaming that started with the box opening. I said, "Jeffrey, let's continue our conversation as we walk. The road is long and hard, and once the sun rises in the sky, the heat will rise."

We made use of a small bag I took from Peterson's house to save water. As we walked, every once in a while, we heard that screaming again.

Jeffrey and I started walking in the desert, leaving behind the river with its many trees. It was a big desert, but we had to get through it if we were to complete our trip. Jeffrey and I began to feel the heat of the scorching sun. We took out the water bag, started drinking water, and continued in the heat. We came to a cliff and lay beneath it so that no one would see us.

A bird passed by in the sky. At first, it was only a black point, and then it was on top of us, but in heaven from afar, as if it looked at us or recognised us. Jeffrey knew it was a falcon because it was high in the sky.

"What does he want in this desert?" I asked. "Is it hunger that brought him here or what?"

Jeffrey said, "Osemer, I do not think hunger is what brought him. I don't think hunger is what he's got. We're not his prey. Someone sent him to find us."

We didn't know what to do or where to hide. "They'll come at any moment," I cried. We start running hard and fast, but we got tired quickly, so we stood a little and looked at the sun in the sky, wondering whether it was about to disappear.

We found a very small cave, but it looked like good shelter for a couple of fugitives. The falcon flew away as if he knew where we were and had made sure that we were the ones he was looking for.

We went back out and finally came to the end of a village, where we found two very old deserted rooms. I broke the door with my feet. We were breathing hard from running a long distance. We did not look around at what was in these two rooms. We were just relieved to find a place to rest. We had crossed half the desert, and we fell into a deep sleep.

I dreamed a dream in which I saw myself with the elder Satan. He was very sick, and I killed him with a dagger in the chest. I woke up in a panic, and I woke up Jeffrey. We were very hungry.

Jeffrey said, "Hey, Osemer, stay here. I'll go get food. Do not come out. We don't know this village."

I told him OK. When he went out of the two old rooms, I saw dim lights there in the house, and I saw some animals that had demons with them. I was looking in the two rooms for a robe to cover me so they wouldn't know me. I found a worn-out robe, and I put it on.

Then I walked into this gathering to find out what was going on. They all wanted to know about this stranger in their little village. I found a dog leaning on the doorstep of the house, as if he was guarding it.

I asked him, "What's going on?"

The dog leaned over the door and said, "You know what's going on."

I walked into the room with the light, and there was an old demon. She said, "Come in."

I said, "What are you doing?"

She said, "I do everything but magic. If you're looking for magic, you won't find it here."

I looked at her for a moment, and then I told her, "I want you to tell me about a dream."

She said, "What is it, boy?"

I didn't tell her I killed a devil in the dream so she wouldn't tell them. Instead, I said, "I saw in a dream that I killed someone with a dagger."

She said, "That means you're going to kill that person, but not with a dagger—with something else. And he knows you're going to kill him, which means you're going to torture him very slowly."

Then I said to her, "Well, thank you."

I went back into our room and found Jeffrey looking upset.

He said, "Osemer, I told you not to go out."

I said, "Yes, but I just went somewhere close—to ask a demon to tell me something. It's not important. Did you bring food?"

He said in an angry tone, "Yes, I got the food."

We went outside behind the room, and I started trying to light a fire to cook the rabbit he brought. Jeffrey started skinning the rabbit. We sat around the fire while the rabbit hung over it, and we flipped it so that the meat was cooked well. The smell of flesh was very tempting for Jeffrey.

CHAPTER 15

I knew very well that this village was small, but we wanted to rest in it one more night before going out in the morning. Maybe the falcon wouldn't come.

At that moment, a very old bear came to us. We greeted him and offered him food, but he said, "I just filled my belly. I'm looking for someone to talk to." Then he started talking.

"I came to this village a long time ago," he began, "and you will find that I am one of the oldest and largest bears in this village. Why won't they make me mayor? Why, why? Is it because I am a bear? They are unjust. I hate them. When I came with my wife and three of our children, no one welcomed us. I built our house myself. Then my wife ran away and took my children with her. She said I talk too much, and I don't shut up. What do you think? This is injustice, isn't it?"

I said, "Yes."

Jeffrey looked at me and then looked at the bear. He wanted to sleep and wished the bear hadn't come.

The bear asked, "May I sleep with you here? I'm alone at home. No one likes me here in the village, and they go to that old hag. I'd rather they came to me and made me the mayor. They'd be better off. This village will regret it. You will see. I am the biggest in this village."

I told him, "Why not go to them and tell them that they are unjust and that you are the best candidate for mayor?" I wanted him to go and not come back. He bothered me, so I started trying to get him to leave.

It was no wonder they wanted to shut him down, but nothing would shut him down but death.

I said, "Bear, why don't you sleep, and then you and I will go early in the morning to the villagers to tell them that you are the best candidate, and that you love this village. Let's sleep now, the better for us to wake up early in the morning.

He said, "You sleep."

I couldn't believe he'd let me sleep, and I was right: he just kept talking. Jeffrey didn't care; he went inside and slept. I stayed, thinking, *Who can make this bear sleep? He speaks and speaks.* After he told me to sleep, he started to speak, and loudly.

"I will make this village the best village in this land. I will make it better than others, and build parks everywhere, build a milk factory of cows and sheep, and make everyone want to live in this village."

I turned my back on him and tried to sleep, but he turned me so he could see my face. What a nuisance!

Then I remembered something. I pulled my bag out. He didn't know what was going on; he just kept speaking. I put a little water in a cup and put in the leaves of the tree that bring sleep. I said, "Bear, take some water and drink. You must be thirsty from talking."

Drinking it, he said, "I will forgive the villagers."

I looked at him and hoped the leaves would start to work soon.

"I'm not going to forgive that old hag, though," he continued. "She's the one who made my wife run away. She was talking to her every day, telling lies about me, and my wife believed her."

The leaves weren't working. I forgot he was a bear. I added more leaves to the water and gave it to him. I said, "Drink to get your throat wet. I see you're tired of talking."

He thanked me and took a drink. He didn't finish ten words before he fell asleep.

CHAPTER 16

I woke up about three hours after the sun came up. I woke Jeffrey up quickly before the bear woke up. We then started out to complete the journey through the great desert. Finally we came across a valley with a dangerous slope, and we started down into it with caution. When we'd passed it, we started with the long, tiring plains. They went on and on. We kept going until our mouths dried up and we couldn't talk from the thirst.

I felt the key moving in my pocket. But why? We were in a barren desert. It emitted wonderful colours, and suddenly it was pointing right.

Jeffrey said, "Look, look!" He pointed to something. We saw something like a hole in the dirt. What, a mirage? That's what it seemed like to us. But as we approached this pit, we saw that it was not a mirage. It was a well in the middle of the desert. There was a bucket attached, as if it was ready for us. I pulled it out to get water, and then I gave it to Jeffrey. When we were finished, there was no water left.

We continued walking until we reached a large mountain. There was a hole in the bottom of this mountain, like a large cave or a coal mine with lights. There were paths left and right and in every direction.

We stood there in the passageway. It was terrifying. There were skulls and bones all over. Someone wanted to scare whoever entered so that they ran out quickly. This indicated that there was something important here. I focused on these things, and soon we saw in the middle of the corridor a medium-sized box and a small skull. I picked up the box and tried to open it.

Jeffrey said, "I saw an axe at the entrance." The entrance was not far from the box, so we went back and grabbed the axe. I brought it back to the box and started trying to break the lock, but my first attempt failed.

"You didn't hit the lock," Jeffrey pointed out.

I got my strength up, lifted the axe, and hit it right on the lock, which broke down into dirt. I took the box in my hands, and I thought it was magic. Inside the box was a piece of paper.

What was that paper? It was not a regular paper. I could barely see what was written on it due to the dirt. I shook the dirt off and saw that it was a map of the mountain. I decided to follow it.

We completed the corridor to the end, and then we came out of the mountain. The mountain, green and vast, separated the desert. In front of it was a big village. When we approached it, we looked closely at it, and it appeared to be a whole demon village with no animals.

I said to Jeffrey, "What do we do now? Our way is over. This is the end. What do we do?"

He said, "Listen: you stay here, and I will go to the village. I'll bring back a robe or blanket for you to wear it."

I told him, "I'll wait for you behind this big rock so that nobody sees me."

When Jeffrey entered the village, everyone looked at him, and some of them were afraid of him. He saw a robe hanging outside a shop. He took it and ran to me. None of them could catch him, since he was running as fast as he could. When he got to me, I put the robe on and wore it, and I made my body look old like I couldn't walk, so we didn't seem suspicious.

The truth is, the demons were stupid. They didn't think very much, and they believed anything. We started crossing the village, and everyone looked at us, but we didn't care, as long as we reached the end of the village.

I started to focus on the map. It was dark outside, so we went inside an empty house. No one could hear us. The whole house was a ladder up and down. We were not interested in the rising stairs. What drew our attention were the stairs down. It took a long time to climb down them. We ended up at a cracked wooden door that was standing open. We pushed it, and it made a strong sound of friction. It had dried up a long time ago and was still stuck to the floor.

The room we entered was full of frozen animals in bottles. We saw some strange movements, and Jeffrey and I were filled with fear and expectation at the same time.

What was this place? I told Jeffrey to stop; I wanted to look at the map. We then found another ladder down, and then a door, and then more bottles. There was no side corridor at all. Some of the bottles had frozen snakes in them. Every frozen animal has a sheet above it showing its age and the date of its freezing and why it was arrested.

As we walked through this long basement, we saw every species of animal, even wolves. But what really surprised me was that there were also frozen demons. Who did this job if not demons? Why would they freeze their own species?

Then I realized that this was a prison. It was the devil's prison in this basement, and the prisoners were frozen.

At the end of the ladder, there was a big bottle of freezing liquid for a new prisoner. I wanted to know who was inside, and I was shocked to see my friend William. He was frozen! William!

"Look, Jeffrey!" I said. "It's William!"

I started reading why he was arrested, and I saw that it was for helping a criminal and sheltering him. I took a fire extinguisher that was hanging and started to hit the glass and hit it hard. But the bottle was strong. It was dedicated to the prison and not regular glass.

Then I heard a voice, and I stopped to hear it well. It was coming from inside the house. Someone was coming from above the basement. I said, "Come on, Jeffrey. Let's hide behind that bottle." There was a big bottle of frozen bear in front of our friend's bottle.

Jeffrey said, "There's a chair in there and a cup of tea on the little table. He's a demon. That means he's fast. We don't want to make any sound."

We saw a demon walking and looking at bottles one after the other and concentrating on every one, looking serious in his work, approaching us, and coming closer. We were at the end of the basement. The demon started to get more focused on the animals. He was afraid one of them might escape. Finally, he arrived before us. I saw him, but he did not see me behind the bottle. He went back and sat in the place where his seat was and started drinking his tea.

After he finished the tea, he walked to the entrance. We watched his body go up the steps until he disappeared. Then we came out of hiding.

I concentrated on the bottle and hit it with my maximum strength. It broke, and water from it filled the floor. William started breathing, but barely. Water was inside his lungs. I started pulling him out of the bottle. I had to put him on the ground. How heavy he was! He began to shiver.

"Settle down!" I said. "I am your friend Osemer."

His eyes were red. I didn't know what else they put in those bottles. I took water out of my purse and put it in his mouth. He couldn't move. He could barely look right and left.

"I am Osemer, your friend," I said. "Did they put something in your head? Have you lost your memory?"

He smiled and said. "Osemer, take me out of here!"

I carried him on my back and began to climb up the exit ladder. We went out, and I was looking for a big rock to sit behind or something. I only found a small slope, but the three of us could hide and lie down. The fresh air had a positive effect, and I noticed the change in my friend's face. He was much better. His hands and legs began to move a little, so I grabbed his hands and made him move them.

CHAPTER 17

We stayed in that place until the sun was gone, and then William could walk and run. We started to complete our journey in the dark. As we walked, William told us what happened to him. After Peterson took office as mayor and started repairing the village and cleaning it, he attracted great interest from the neighbouring villages. He worked on the fountain, and the news went out to all the distant and neighbouring villages. Other villagers started coming, one after the other, until the last village came.

"One of the visitors saw me, and he knew me. I was looking at him, and he was talking to the man next to him, whispering in his ear. I ran away, and they all ran after me until I was tired. They caught me, and they put me in jail. That means we're close to the vault."

I asked him, "Did they torture you?"

"They didn't torture me. They put me in that glass bottle. You feel like you are in a dream, and in another life."

The question in my mind was how we had followed the map until we found our friend. That meant someone knew where our friend was imprisoned. Or maybe it was just a coincidence. Either option could true, but I had to focus on these things. Demons knew how to put up tricks and traps.

I said to my friends, "Listen, no one leaves. We stay together so that no one gets caught."

We found a small hill with soft soil, and we lay in the soft dirt. All of us slept a deep sleep, but I was afraid of the key. It had started to shine, and I was afraid someone would come and take it while we were asleep. I hid it in a bag to stop it from shining.

I looked at my friends, and each of them was asleep because of his hard work. I put the bag next to me, and I went to sleep too.

We slept the whole night, and the sun woke us up. Flies covered our faces. We got up quickly and gathered our scattered things. I saw the key on the ground away from where I had been sleeping. I must have thrown it.

We took everything and started walking. I held the key in my hand. I wrapped it in my hand so hard, my hand was like a square. When I opened my hand, the key pointed in the direction of a mountain to the northeast of our location. It was like it wanted to show us something.

We went in the direction of the key, and the key turned green. I didn't know what it meant, but it had meaning. It was one colour and bright. I'm sure it meant something.

There was actually a series of conjoined mountains, but the one we wanted was the largest. We started climbing and climbing. Soon we were hungry, and the sun was hot on our heads. I didn't know what I was looking for until we found the thing that we wanted in this extreme heat, that we needed in the desert, that we loved at the farm. The magnificent mountain, all in the shade and open air, was blooming with all sorts of fruits, not cultivated but natural. Cultivated fruits are neat and small; these were large and scattered.

With my eyes, I savoured this wonderful bounty. I was filled with hunger. I started to run to the food and forgot my friends. I was not going to leave a twig. I ran next to the grape tree and stayed in the palm of the banana tree.

I knew now what the key was all about. It was not a trick or a plot, but a key that helped its owner. Not everyone could carry it. As soon as I caught it, it lit up. The green colour symbolized something great, and the red colour symbolized the devil and evil and every trick and intrigue. I put the key in my pocket, and I went to find water.

As my friends drank, I sat next to them. I drank and drank until my thirst was quenched. Then I run to the apple tree and next to it the oranges, and I started eating apples. This tree was watered by the water of gold. I ate about five apples.

My friends were lying under the grapes. I was amazed by their lack of hunger. They were all the time thirsty but not hungry.

I left them continued to fill my belly. Then I went to lay down with them, and I brought some apples and oranges. I said to William, I said, "When do you want to go? I will collect as many fruits as I can in this beautiful place. Don't you eat fruit, William, you devil?

He said, "I do eat it, Osemer, but it tastes in our mouths not as it does to you humans. We are denying it a little bit, but in the extreme of hunger, we eat lest we die, so the need justifies the means."

"You are strange things, you devils. Your prisons are weird, yet you have better land than ours. You kill, you charm, you do everything bad. You don't know the value of these precious things. What a waste. Because of your extravagance, you do not deserve this land."

I went on, "Let this earth go so don't you destroy the animals and put them in jail. Leave this land to the animals. They are more wise than you, and they deserve to govern this land. But you will not leave it, because you are a bad leader and a big demon. Your master sends demons to exterminate what he wants and what he desires, but he waits for me to kill him. They deserve it, and they will be judged by either a fair lion or a wise Jeffrey or even an honourable bear. Remember my words, William: if no one stops him, the villages will perish. The animals don't want to start attacking you, and that's what makes them smart and better than you."

Then we woke Jeffrey up and told him, "We want to leave before nightfall."

CHAPTER 18

Jeffrey got up, and we collected all our stuff. We drank until we were stuffed and packed with water. William also filled his bag with water, and we left this wonderful beauty behind. I collected as much fruit as I could.

From the top of the mountain, we could see almost all the valleys and villages around us. We saw parties of villagers in the fog. We were at the top of the mountain and the fog blocked our view, but we could see a little distant village. Then we started to go down, step by step, as the sun began to subside from our shoulders.

When I looked again, it seemed that this village had no desert behind it, as if it was beyond the last of these deserts. But we encountered some valleys that seemed to me to be dangerous. Jeffrey said, "Don't be afraid. We are three, and we are close to the valley with the long walls."

The valley we were in had no long walls, and those who descended from it fell and were killed. There was only one corridor to go down in this strange valley. It was so narrow and small that if we had a bear with us, I don't think it would get through.

We finished coming down, and now we wanted to pass to the other side. There was no corridor. We walked forward a distance of fifty metres and were surrounded by tall grass everywhere. We passed horrible weeds, and we met with fangs, like the fangs of a lion. We passed by, step by step, so he did not feel us, and finally we passed through the valley. We drank the water we had brought with us. The sunset was very beautiful, and then we were walking in darkness.

We were exhausted and tired, so we stopped when we reached a village. I don't know how, but I knew it was not an animal village but a demon village. There was a radiant light in the sky. We hid behind a tree and took out a robe so I would be fully covered and they wouldn't know me.

We took the necessary precautions, and then we started to go to this village, which seemed to be the mother village of this land. It was very big and took the whole valley. We passed old houses and small houses. Half of them were ruined, but I wanted to hide in one. Jeffrey and William went to explore the things of the village, and I sat alone and waited for them until I slept. The air was hot and the lights were not strong, and I wanted to sleep hard. I slept for some time, and when I awoke, they still hadn't returned.

Finally they came back. I asked Jeffrey, "What happened to you? Why did you take so long?"

He said, "I know something about this village. It is the village of the elder master demon. Here there is also a committee of witchcraft and demons. I didn't let them see me. I expected that their master is here because of the size of this village."

Suddenly, as I spoke with Jeffrey, the key in my pocket lit up, and I took it out. It was glowing red.

"That means there's evil coming, or you're in an evil area," Jeffrey said.

We still had to wait for William, so Jeffrey continued with his story. "They were standing in the bar, and there was a great magician who started to tell them about you, as if he knew you. He said, 'It is necessary to kill Osemer. Our master is in a very bad condition. His body is cracked and flabby, and the disease has intensified. You can see Osemer in his eyes and his body. Osemer walks and pulls death behind him. The master's consciousness is over, all because of the vault Osemer opened.' They're looking for you with a grudge and hatred. They even look behind trees. They think humans are stupid. So what do we do now, Osemer?"

I said, "Their master is sick, and we need to kill him by looking for the second vault."

"I think we should start looking in this village," said Jeffrey. "I expect the vault is here. All of them went out to search for you."

We started a search of our own. I went into the house next to me and started looking and looking for any evidence. I found nothing—only white leaves and old yellow ones. There was a basement, and I went down into it, wondering if it could be a trap or a plot. I saw only crushed glass and a lot of garbage and clothes in that basement. I didn't find anything interesting.

I left the house and sat in the dark outside. I thought, *It's about time my friends come for me. Maybe they found the vault.* I waited in the dark until Jeffrey came to me.

"What happened?" I asked. "Did you find it?"

He said, "Unfortunately, Osemer I did not find it. After all this searching, I do not think it exists in the first place. We searched all the village and found no trace of it."

I said, "Don't worry, it exists. I expect William will find it. Wait for him; he may come at any moment. I feel it close to me. Have patience."

After a long while, William came. "Did you find it, William?" I asked.

"No, I didn't find it, Osemer."

I was so sad. I sat down and started to think about where it could be. After a long thought, I felt the key start moving in my pocket, so I pulled it out. It glowed green and pointed to a nearby house. We entered, and it was wonderful what happened to me immediately after entering the basement.

There was no wood floor; it was dirt. I walked and walked, holding the key and looking where it pointed. It point at the ground. There were several holes in the basement, and we started digging and digging until we saw the vault. How beautiful it was! We dug the dirt around it to get it out.

I said, "Come on, pull up with your full power! Come on, let's get it out. It's so beautiful. That's why they buried it, because it's beautiful."

It was decorated in all colours and had some great graphics. I couldn't wait to open it. I took the key out, and it started showing us the same colour as the safe. I placed it in the lock and then the door opened. At first, all I saw was gold and silver jewellery. But this was not what I was looking for. I was looking for secrets.

I saw hidden behind the gold a box that was half black, half studded with gold. When I opened it, I heard screams that filled this whole land and terrified me.

CHAPTER 19

We went out into the village and saw their master on the ground dead. William took me and went to the centre of the witches and demons committee. This place was the centre of evil on this earth, and we walked right in. The evil ones died, but the good people and the animals did not. The village smelled of death.

Our three-way journey continued, with Jeffrey on my right and William on my left. The sun had brightened. We came into some dense trees, and fog was everywhere, so I asked Jeffrey to lead us. He came back to us running like he found something. He said, "I found a room surrounded by trees."

The room had a long black chimney. We knocked on the door once and twice, but no one answered. We opened the door a little and heard a squeaking sound. We entered and saw that it had a small lounge with a table and a bathroom, but there was under our feet the sound of wood, like it was about to fall down and away. We found a small door and opened it. I went down alone, because the stairs were worn, and I found all manner of bread, meat, water, and many other things. We rushed to the well-covered water containers, and after we had finished the water, Jeffrey went to the meat, and William and I went to the bread and cheese. We ate and ate and ate until we couldn't walk.

Then we fell asleep. When I awoke, I felt the darkness on my face.

"Wake up, get up!" I said to my companions. I wanted to climb the next mountain so I could see around me. We stood at the highest point, and the sound of the wind was very high.

At the top of the mountain, we found the entrance to a large cave, like an underground pit. We entered, thinking, *What's in this strange land?* We noticed a strange and unpleasant smell, and when we got to the source of it, we found rotting bodies.

I looked to my right side and saw hand-carved cabins inside the cave. Coming out of them were screaming and crying sounds. I moved forward quickly until we got to a crossroads. We found there a plaque with old blood on it.

To the right or to the left? We decided to go to the right, because the left looked like a dead-end. We found a prison that was also hand-carved and had a rusty gate, and there were more bodies inside the cells.

William said, "Get out! This place is not good. It's not what we're looking for."

Going out now was a loss, to my mind, since we had only just started to make our discoveries. Jeremy agreed with me, so it was the two of us against William. The cave was a maze, with turns at the end of every corridor.

We heard a voice as we came to the end of one corridor. There we found a small hole in the corner of the corridor almost unseen to the eye. We couldn't crawl through it, so we started looking for anything that would help us finish digging this hole.

I found a buried plank covered with sand. I took it, and I called to William and Jeremy. They came quickly—they thought I had something. I said, "William, grab this plank and start hitting the hole. Watch out; don't break the plank."

The corridor was old and shaking on top of us, with grains of sand coming down. We were afraid it would fall down on us. I finished digging the hole after William got tired, and the hole was ready to crawl into.

At first, I feared that there would be someone inside the pit. Jeremy crawled in first to check it out. Then Jeffrey came out and William crawled in. The pit was not big, but it was big enough for the three of us. So we all crawled in, and we realized that we were under the cave entrance. When we emerged, there were lights all around; it was radiant like a city. We made our way toward the lights, and we heard more voices as we went.

I said to my friends, "Stop! My foot is bleeding."

They sat with me, and William took out a first-aid bag he'd taken from the medicine in the cave. It stopped the bleeding, but I was lame.

We could see the end of the road, and it was strange that the end was dark despites the lights of the city. As we approached, we found flowers and fruit. There was a giant apple tree, so we put a few apples in our bags. Two hikers came to us, and they were so weird, I didn't know what they were. They were wearing a blanket around them, and I couldn't figure out if they were animals or demons. They both carried axes.

Once of them said, "Who are you?"

I answered, "I am Osemer, and this is William, and this is Jeffrey."

"Why are you here?"

I said, "We are travellers, and we don't know what this place is."

One of the hikers, named Al-qusayr, said, "Beware the outskirts of the city. It is better to enter the city quickly."

We came close to the city, and the strange thing was that the lights were bright, yet we didn't see anyone when we entered the city at nine o'clock at night. We walked and walked until we reached the heart of the city.

"Now we have to decide which section we will choose," I said. "Which side do you want, William?"

Before he answered, we heard screams from the left side, so we went to the right and started walking. Suddenly, a big rabbit came out of a house waving at us to come in.

We went to him, and I said, "I'm Osemer, and these are my friends William and Jeffrey."

"My name is John," said the rabbit. "I will give you everything you desire and need."

There was a bruise on his left cheek and he was very skinny, despite all the food and drink in the very large house. He gave each of us our own room on the ground floor. I noticed that I stopped limping the moment I entered this house.

There was no one in the house other than this bunny. I wished to ask him many questions, but I was very tired of traveling, so I did not hesitate to go to bed. I fell into a deep sleep and slept until I was awakened by the smell of the delicious breakfast and a knock on the door of my room.

"Breakfast is ready," said John. He woke William and Jeffrey, and we started to eat breakfast.

CHAPTER 20

We went out with John after breakfast, and there was a big masquerade going on. It was the biggest celebration I'd ever seen. I started rushing and laughing with the crowd and running around. Jeffrey and William stayed with John, who was throwing firecrackers everywhere.

Suddenly, I saw an arrow hit a very fat squirrel in front of me. I didn't know what was going on, but I quickly went to the squirrel. He was down on the ground, and blood was gushing out. Jeffrey came to help me.

The squirrel's face was familiar to me, like I had seen him somewhere in a village we went through. I took him to John's house.

"What happened?" asked John.

"This squirrel got hit," I said. I was surprised at how much blood the squirrel had lost. I thought he wouldn't survive.

But John came with a disinfectant, a first-aid kit, and a cloth. He asked the squirrel to bite the cloth. We put the disinfectant on the wound on his chest, and he started screaming from the pain. I dressed the wound, and then we let him rest in a room opposite from my room.

We went down the hall, and I felt there was something John wasn't telling me. I didn't want to ask him in front of everyone. We sat talking in the hall about the beauty of this city. Actually, *we* didn't talk. John was the one who talked to us.

Finally, I said, "John, I want to get some sleep." I went to my room. William was left with John. In fact, though, I didn't want to sleep; I wanted to talk to the squirrel, but I was hesitant. I entered my room a bit, trying to figure out what to say. I knew the squirrel was going to tell me something, but I didn't know what it was.

Eventually I got my nerve up and went and knocked on his door. Then I entered. I did not wait. The floor of the house was old, and the floor creaked as I walked.

I saw him look my way, and I said, "Hi. I am Osemer."

He said, "I'm Martin."

"Who did this to you?" I asked. It was a stupid question. How would he know?

But he said, "We have problems in every celebration when a crowd comes out."

I asked him, "Will you be making a response?"

He said, "Osemer, we don't know who shot the arrow, and if we knew, I couldn't catch him here."

I got curious and asked, "Why can't you catch him and know who he is?"

He just told me go and sleep a little. "You've had a busy day."

I said, "I'll be in my room if you need anything. It's right across the hall."

"I know what room you and your friends are in," he said.

I went to my room, but I didn't feel like sleeping. Looking out the window, I saw a car standing in front of the house. John was talking to someone.

CHAPTER 21

When morning finally came, I wanted to go out, so I went down the hall and found John and William.

John said, "Let's go to my friend Frank's house."

We started walking, and it was a long, hard road. The sun rose, and the earth was cold. Trees lined the passageways to Frank's house.

John said to me, "Osemer, you'll know everything soon. Don't rush."

There was a big gate with four guards in front of us. The guards searched us, and then one guard said, "Are you carrying anything, Osemer?"

How did he know my name? I wondered.

They opened the gate for us, and we walked through a vast garden on the way to a house. We were received by a man who said, "Welcome, guests, please come in." We walked behind him for a long time inside the house until he took us to an underground room. He stood at the door and said, "I can't go into this room, but Frank welcomes you."

John knocked on the door. A big voice said, "Enter." We entered the room and saw an old man sitting in a chair and leaning on his right side, as if he was injured. He could barely talk. He said to me, "Osemer, has anyone told you why are you here?"

I told him no.

He said. "Do you know why Martin was injured yesterday?"

Again, I said no.

"I'll tell you, Osemer. It's clear that your heart is good, so please understand what I'm saying. This land has two faces, and now you see the first face. The other side—the left—are our enemies, although not all of them. They have a leader named Seymour. He is the head of evil. If we kill him, evil may stop forever.

He continued, "If you want to be with us, there's no way back. John will tell you everything, so don't be hasty."

Then John rose up, and I walked with him out of the room. He said, "Come with me behind the house." He led us to an area well covered with trees where a large group of animals had gathered. It appeared that John knew them. Gesturing to us, he said to them, "These are new members. This is Osemer, and this is William."

Then he introduced us to the others. Leonard was tall, and his body was big. David had average-length hair up to his eyes; he was smart, and he planned everything. Linda was obviously in love with David, and he was holding her hand. Robert had a face that made me think he was a lunatic. There were a lot of them, but there wasn't enough time for John to introduce them all.

We sat on the ground, and David started showing us some of the wanted figures from the left side. They had a dark history, and they had long been hunted. "We have not been able to arrest them yet," said John.

David said. "This is Seymour, the leader of the evil, and this is James, who is close to Seymour and his favourite. He's our biggest wanted after Seymour killed almost twenty of us. That's the approximate number we think he killed, but I'm sure, personally, he's killed a lot more than that. We can catch James through Thomas; he's the little brother. This is Fred, the mastermind. This is their map, and this is Joey, the executor of cunning and deceitful movements, like what happened yesterday with Martin. I think he did it."

He continued, "This is Roy. He is simple, tall, with a big body. He is our problem in battles. This is Louis. He is the maker of armour and swords and arrows. But of course, he is not alone. He has someone with him who helps him out."

David sat down after he was finished. I started thinking about how long this conflict had been going on and what would happen if we won. What happened if Frank died suddenly? He was old, and he could barely talk. Any bad news could kill him.

We followed Stephen to another room through a narrow, water-filled corridor. Stephen said, "Here we are. Beware of the water." He opened the door to the room.

There were dangerous pieces of iron scattered everywhere. I reached for a piece of curved iron, and Stephen called out, "Be careful, Osemer!"

When we got to the end of the room, we sat on a couch. Stephen started explaining what we were seeing. "This room was made by Frank and his old friends," he said, "and yesterday was a great celebration that Martin had to pay for. Frank, the oldest and most experienced of us, has been involved in more than thirty battles, some in the city and some in villages, and he is now injured. They have tried to kill him several times. This room was made fights and for making weapons, developing them, and running experiments."

They start showing us things like a small rounded shield for running or using a sword and a big heavy shield for those who use arrows. You could put arrows in the shield. There were four types of arrows, Stephen explained. "Narcotic stocks, where we putting some kind of alcohol in it so we can catch the guy alive; toxic stocks, and for this type of use we have the opposite (left) type; the common stock, which contains nothing and rarely kills; and blazing arrows, on which we light alcohol to burn enemy tents or scare the enemy in case they are more than us."

He went on, "The swords are what we focus on as our basic weapon. The enemy is very sophisticated in the field of swords. They have two kinds of swords: the little sword for dodging in manual combat and a big heavy sword. We are trying hard to develop our swords, but most of the time we defeat our enemies with arrows. Always they are more than us in number."

He added, "We have a weapon that we're working on—a new one that the enemy does not have, a four-wheeled mobile cannon. So far, we have no ammunition. We are working to make ammo in a mountain behind the city. This mountain contains dynamite. These are all our weapons so far."

CHAPTER 22

David said he would take us to an area called Tal. We went out the back of the city and faced a lake. We were still surrounded by trees.

Robert said, "I can't go on. You know what happened last time we went through here. Who wants to go back with me?"

Everyone was silent in amazement. Nobody knew what he meant by what happened last time—at least, I didn't know.

"Well, I'm going," said Robert. "See you later. We don't want this anyway. It's always like this; it's cold, and the fog covers the lake."

David led the way. Linda was holding his coat and looked scared. We passed the lake. Stephen said, "The lake is just a little in front of what we're going to bring you to." David was sure of himself and walked without hesitation.

William said, "I'm tired. I want to rest a little bit."

David said, "Okay, guys. We're going to take a little break. Five minutes, no more. This road is controlled and risky. Enemies know we have something in this place, so as much as you can, hurry up."

We sat in a circle, and everyone started talking about themselves.

David said, "I blew up my house when I was a kid. I couldn't find my dad, and I stayed in the rubble half a day until Frank came and took me and raised me. He trained me in archery, swords, and all sorts of fighting."

Stephen said, "I'm a big dealer. I trade in anything, and I have a big farm. Frank came to me wanting to buy iron I was selling at the cheapest prices. I didn't know why, and I was encouraging him to become a big trader. I think because he was smart."

He went on, "I knew he was making armour, but I didn't know why. I was bored with solitude and loneliness, so I asked people about his house, and I went to him. He told me everything, and I respected his desire and his direction. He might know how to convince people. I didn't know David was not the real son of Frank at that point."

Leonard said, "I was looking for money. I was in the most need of money. My father was old, and he had worked enough. My mother woke up early in the morning, washed clothes, and cooked for us. My sister, Marie, helped her. She's still learning every day. My dad feels a little shortness of breath sometimes. My mom makes medicine from herbs."

Linda said, "My home is next to Frank's house. I looked out the window every day to see David. I loved him from the very first moment I saw him. I was young, and he too was young." She smiled, and David laughed. Then she continued, "One day, he went out on a picnic with Frank. When Frank got busy with the ice cream salesman, I ran up to David and grabbed his hand."

Mark said, "I am a simple man from a simple family. I love laughing and taking joy in everything and anything. I am rarely sad. The times go by, and I don't remember much. Sometimes I try to learn, but I rarely get serious. I like walking from place to place when everyone is asleep."

It was William's turn to speak. "My story is complicated," he said, "but I'll tell it the best I can. I knew Osemer's father, August. He was my friend and older than me. When he died, he asked that I stay with Osemer."

David said, "Let's go. We're late. We've taken a lot of time. We don't want to go back. The sun is shining, so it's dangerous for us."

We continued our journey. I was walking behind Sandy, and she kept looking at me and smiling. The road was dark, cold, and fog-covered. I could see a distance of twenty metres from the road. Sometimes we could not see each other in the fog.

"What happened here?" I asked.

In a faint voice, William said, "I don't know, Osemer. I don't know."

It appeared that there had been a massacre, and it was definite and curious that everyone was ready to fight. Clara was equipped with arrows, and Leonard was holding his sword. Everyone was on alert.

Suddenly, the earth ended in a steep slope. Mark said, "This is my favourite part. Let's run fast down the slope."

Leonard and Stephen ran with him. I was next to David until we got to a big lighthouse, but we didn't need the lights at the moment. The dawn was about to come, and the sky was blue and clear, but the fog was still upon us.

The dawn breeze began to sweep the fog away. We sat out of fatigue around the plank. Lying on my back, I looked at the clear sky. It was an unforgettable moment. Sandy sat next to me and grabbed my hand. She surprised me. I looked at Clara, who was looking angrily at Sandy.

David said, "I'm going first." With Linda and Stephen, he ran under a rope and into the lighthouse. The rope went back into the ground, and it was tied to a flat plank. In fact, it was a moving plank, running from the ground to the lighthouse. If you pulled the other rope up to the lighthouse, the first rope brought you back to earth. They went up and lit the light at the top of the lighthouse.

Leonard said, "I'm going to go, Osemer."

William and I joined him and started to climb up the plank. Suddenly, I felt the plank shake under Leonard's huge body. I felt like it wasn't going to hold us. William and I backed down the plank, frightened until we returned to earth. After that, we went two by two; the plank couldn't accommodate three people. I went up again with William.

When we got to the top, we found big and small binoculars. It was a surveillance centre where we could see any part of the city. Everyone took turns looking through Mark's telescope.

"Look at that bakery," he said. "It's crowded. The line is as long as this lighthouse."

Stephen said, "That's my farm! Come on, Osemer, and look at my farm." He gave me his telescope, and I looked through. I saw the big farm we went through before we entered the city.

I asked him, "Who are the two people in it?"

He said, "They are guards who work for me to protect the farm from burning crops and stealing."

We started climbing down, and I was the last to come down. Now I knew why they had made us come so far from the city—because of this magnificent beacon for observation. As we made our return along the uphill slope, a wagon stopped by. The driver was old, and he didn't care about our number or who we were. He was happy to give us a ride.

The old man drove us very fast. David tried to explain to him where we were going, and when he finally mentioned Frank, the old man said, "Why didn't you tell me Frank's house? I live in the last row of houses, and I've known Frank since he was young. He doesn't remember me. He was one of my friends. We played together."

When we got to Frank's house, we were shown to our rooms. My room was opposite Clara's and beside Sandy's. I entered my room and fell to the bed in a deep sleep.

CHAPTER 23

I was awakened by a knocking on the door. I was deeply fatigued and tried to ignore it, but then I heard Sandy's voice saying, "Open up, Osemer! Quickly, before anyone sees me."

I was scared, so I quickly opened the door. Sandy had cooked me breakfast. It smelled delicious. I knew she liked me.

She said, "What do you think of my cooking, Osemer?"

I said, "I'm embarrassed."

It was eggs with a little cheese and hot bread and some fruit. I wanted Sandy to understand that I admired her. I got up and gave her some of the food.

Suddenly, I remembered something. Jeffrey! We had left him behind. He must be wondering what happened to us. I bolted out of the room, with Sandy calling out behind me, "Wait, Osemer! I want to tell you something. Wait!"

I didn't wait. I ran out of the mansion. The gate was locked, and the guards were suspicious of me. John came out running after me.

"Hey, Osemer, wait!" he called out. "Why this speed? Your friend is safe. He's in my house.

I stopped then.

John said, "We will go and bring him with us."

I said, "I can't believe I forgot about him, John."

"We all forgot," he said.

It was raining, and the road was full of water, but we could run in it. Finally, we reached the house. I opened the door and called out, "Jeffrey! Jeffrey, where are you?"

There was no response.

John went looking in the back of the house, and I went upstairs where we had been sleeping. I kept calling out, "Jeffrey, it's Osemer! Can you hear me?"

A crackling sound started small and grew and grew. I started walking slowly to the hallway upstairs where my room had been, and something strange happened: the darkness of the hallway intensified, and lights started flashing on and off. I had to stop because I couldn't see anything.

The door to Jeffrey's room was a little open. I pushed it, and it made a loud and annoying sound. The room was empty. Jeffrey's bed looked slept on, but Jeffrey was not there. I searched under the bed. The room was not big, and it was clear that Jeffrey was not in it.

The crackling sound continued and was as sharp as an undertow. The sound came from the ground floor. I left Jeffrey's room, and I bumped into John at the door

"I didn't find him," he said, anticipating my question. "Osemer, you go to the ground floor. I'll look upstairs.

"Wait, John," I called out. "What's that sound?"

John said, "Don't worry, Osemer. Maybe it is air coming through some of the windows or doors."

I went to search for my friend, and I thought desperately, *If I didn't find him in his room, where will I find him? And if I find him, what am I going to tell him? We all forgot about him! Well, it doesn't matter. What matters is that I'm going to apologize to him. If I know Jeffrey, that will be enough.*

I searched the ground floor. The sound was getting closer. There was a mumbling of voices, but I didn't hear what they were saying. The lounge was on my left, and there was a room with one number. I thought it was John's room, but I wasn't sure. I went across a long portico. The hallway to the end was dark, and all civilizations had passed that place. It was evidence of John's great age.

There was a picture in a dark part of the hallway that wasn't clear. I put my hand on the picture, and I found blood on my hands. I wiped my hand with some cloth I was wearing, and then I realized, "John gave it to me."

Finally, I got to the pit—a dark hole with a ladder you can't see the end of it. I was curious. I wanted to know what was down there. Maybe Jeffrey fell in this hole. I started going down, worried that I didn't know the end of it.

CHAPTER 24

There was a smell of rotting blood. The floor of was made of dirt. This pit was not part of the house; the house was part of the pit, and the house was built for the pit. No one came in this pit, or at least cleaned it up.

I followed a lot of corridors, and finally I was standing in the middle. John had never told me about the enormity of this pit. There were even some rusty swords and arrows. I knew that this place had a history—that this pit had seen battles.

I took the corridor in front of me. There was someone here; I was sure of it. I started looking for him. I saw a blood line on the dirt, and I kept following it until I got to a big door made of wood. I opened it and stuck my head in a little.

I saw someone sitting in front of the wall of dirt. His back was to the door, and his face was to the wall. There was a vast area between him and the door, and his back was strangely twisted. He looked like he was waiting for something. Then he turned to me. He was very ugly and had a big beard. His hands were tied with iron, and the iron was fixed to the wall. He spoke to me loudly, but I did not understand what he mumbled.

I looked at him in amazement. I didn't know what to do or what to say. Suddenly, I heard John coming.

"Hey, Osemer, where are you?" he called out. "What are you doing? You shouldn't come down here. This is a forbidden area for new members like you. This area will be the last thing you learn with us, not the first."

He went on, "We didn't find your friend. Let's go back to Frank's mansion now."

I said, "We'd better wait here for a few days. Maybe Jeffrey ..."

I noticed that John was afraid to come near this man. I could see it in his eyes. He shook his head and led me back upstairs.

John went to the kitchen next to the lounge. I sat down thinking about the guy in the basement. John came with two cups of tea. I tasted it a little bit and put it aside to ask him, "John, who's this guy downstairs?"

John said, "He got into a fight with us. He is from the enemies on the left side. It was the biggest battle for us in terms of booty and captives, and what we gained from the battle were the biggest and most important spoils we got. We call it the battle of the mountain. It's where the Red Mountain became the colour of blood. We won that fight, and our dead were a little bit compared to theirs.

"It was the first time we benefited from our equipment hidden in the mountain," John went on. "Even Frank was with us in that fight. This guy in the basement is Cedric. He planned and prioritized everything for their side. He chose the weapons they used. I hit him in the battle, but they shot Clara. Still, we got him where we wanted him, and we planned to catch him in battle and get him to tell us everything we need to defeat the evil on the left."

He continued, "This is Cedric, who didn't think we were going to catch him. This is Cedric, who killed a lot of us—not in battles, but in assassinations he was organizing. He is refusing to confess, refusing to give us anything. Some members beat him up a little during the interrogation. They were so angry at Cedric. He destroyed houses. He did not differentiate between male or female or small or big.

"He has gone crazy in the basement out of solitude and loneliness. He has lost hope of getting out. He is afraid we will not feed him but let him starve. We offered Cedric the chance to be with us, and we would release him. But he stays loyal his group, even if they are corrupt."

Then John said, "I'm tired, and I want to sleep. See you later, Osemer."

CHAPTER 25

John went to sleep in his room in front of the lounge. I was sitting on a sofa, and I fell asleep there. It was four o'clock in the afternoon, and it was a deep slumber.

In my sleep, I dreamt of Jeffrey telling me, "Come on, Osemer." There was a beautiful view behind the river, and the fog spread over the place from the cooler river. There was a small hut and the smell of barbecue. I started to walk in the dream. I entered the river. It was very cold, and there were fishes around my feet. Then I fell off the couch.

My head hurt, and I thought, *Is this a dream? I wish it was a fact. I wish it didn't end.* I got up and fell again. My feet were cold, as if I had entered a real river. This was strange, for at the time I woke up in the middle of the night, the house was warm. I wrapped cloth around my feet, and then I walked down the hallway and went to the pit. I found no ladder; I think John removed it. I had to find another way to go down.

I went straight to the kitchen. There was so much equipment in the kitchen, I was sure I would find something to help me. I started opening everything up. In the third drawer on my right, I found a long rope. I tied the rope to me, and I tied the other end to a hanging lamp in the wall near the pit. The rope was long, and I started to descend. The dirt on the floor of the pit was cold.

I stood a little behind the door, and I heard Cedric mumbling like he was talking to someone. He said a few words that I understood, but the majority of words he couldn't pronounce. I pushed the door a little bit; he heard the sound and stopped mumbling. Then I went in. Leaving some distance between him and me, I began to walk towards him. He was very quiet and astonished.

When the distance between him and me was two metres, I said, "Hello. I am Osemer."

He shook his head.

I didn't know what to say. Finally I told him, "I was walking down the corridors, and I thought I'd come and talk to you a little while."

He shook his head again. I was not looking at him as much as I could, because he was ugly. His ears were big, and he had a very scary nose.

I said, "How long have you been in jail here, Cedric?"

He was trying to talk hard, opening his whole mouth. In a loud and intense voice, he stammered, "I was ... I can ... Talk ... even ... I got it."

I said, "Don't worry. I don't care."

He held up three fingers on his hand to indicate that he had been there three years. Then he smiled and said, "None of my friends or people knew I was alive. If they knew, they would come for me."

I said, "Cedric, they left you on the battlefield. You were injured, and they left you there." I tried to make him forget them and ally with us. I began to make him not only forget them but also hate them. "Why did they not look for your body if they thought you were killed on the battlefield?"

He was silent. I told him to think well, and I would come to him in the morning. I went out using the rope. My clothes were full of dirt. I went to my room to find something to wear. The closet was filled with worn and old clothes. Some were not clean, but I found an old coat that was. I put it on and went straight out.

CHAPTER 26

It was three o'clock in the morning, but I wanted to get some fresh air. The sky was clear blue, and the stars were beginning to disappear. It was a beautiful view.

John's house was on a main street on the right side overlooking a big street, if not the biggest street. On the right, I saw a baby statue pointing his hand to the left. I walked to the left, and there were very few houses on that side, but I kept walking until nothing was left but desert.

Under the shining moonlight, I entered the desert. There was a paved road to follow. I looked behind me and saw the city's lights fading farther away.

I walked a long distance. When I saw a small hole with pure water, I drank from it. Then I continued my march into the unknown until I was about to fall.

The path ended up in a valley—a long rectangle—and I saw that it was full of small tents. Some were lit up. I saw other people lying outside without tents. The valley was crowded with people.

Suddenly, I realized what was going on.

In the valley was a source of water. I saw animals packing cans with water and going to the tents. I went to the source and approached a duck with a long beak. "Hello!" I said.

The duck replied, "Hello."

I asked, "What's going on here?"

The duck said, "What do you see? Just gathering water." In a tone of anger and ridicule, she said, "Sleep well. Tomorrow, we have a lot of work to do."

The duck went to the tents. I saw a cat walk out of a small lean-to, dragging his feet on the ground like he was so tired he could barely make it upstream. I asked him, "Hey, Kitty, what's going on here?"

The cat said, "Tomorrow is the beginning of the end. The battle is well prepared. Take as much water as you can. You'll need it during the battle."

He bent over to pack the water. I froze in my place for a moment, and then I went back and started climbing out of the valley. The dirt at the edge of the valley was very hard to climb, but I was able to run to the city. I went in a hurry to John's house to tell him about this. Tired of running, I sat down a little in front of the city lights. My feet were hurting from climbing out of the valley.

After a moment, I got up and ran a little more until I got to the outskirts of the city where the small houses were. I nearly collided with a baby out on the street. "Come, son," I said. I grabbed his small hand, and I started knocking on doors, asking, "Is this your son?" Finally I came to a very small house; it was mostly underground, though the façade was above the ground.

"Hey, is this your son?" I asked.

A monkey opened the door and said, "Yes, yes! Where did you find him?"

I said, "In the middle of the road."

The monkey said, "Thank you! Here, drink some coffee with us."

I told him, "I can't. I'm in a hurry."

Then I give him his son, and I ran fast until I got to the statue. I went right, and John's house was in front of me, and the night was over.

CHAPTER 27

I went straight through the hall to John's room. I banged on John's door and said, "John, hurry!"

I heard John's voice saying, "What do you want? I'm sleeping! Come back in an hour."

I kept banging. "John, open the door quickly!"

John opened the door and looked at me with one eye open and the other closed. "What is it, Osemer?" he said sleepily.

I said, "Get up. I saw in the desert valley many tents."

"And what else?"

"I asked someone what was going on. He told me to get ready for battle tomorrow."

John said, "Battle? What? Come on, we're going to Frank's house. Just let me give Cedric his food." We went quickly to Cedric and gave him his food—some hot bread, eggs, and cheese in a big bowl. We were in a hurry. We went down to the pit by the rope I had put in the night before. I assumed John was going to ask me about the rope I put in to go to Cedric, but he didn't.

When we got to Frank's house, the guards knew John and opened the gate. I stood a little tired in the garden, and John ran to the balcony, crying, "Tell everyone in the palace to wake up."

Everyone around me was running into the palace. I knew there would be a fight. Everyone was running one way: to the gun room. I saw David walking very quietly out of Frank's room, taking instructions. Weapons were everywhere, including swords and arrows made for the enemy. William was holding arrows and running around with everyone. He did not pay attention to me.

Finally, John said, "Osemer, come. Come on, pick your weapon."

I saw Stephen, Mark, Leonard, David, and Linda all gathering their weapons. Some of them wore armour and were ready to go out, and some of them were still preparing their arrows. Sandy came to me with a bow and arrows, but I didn't want arrows. I wanted a sword

I picked up a big sword, but I could not carry it. It was too heavy. Clara gave me a longer but lighter sword. I wanted to ask her about the battle—how the enemy would attack. But she was not talking to anyone. Everybody was scared of her, or she didn't like anyone.

We all took our weapons and declared a state of war in the area. Frank said that everyone should fight who wanted to defend his home and his money. The animals came out of their houses heading to Frank's house. They took up their guns and followed David. Everyone followed David.

David asked me to show him where I had seen the tents. He wanted to surprise the enemy where they slept rather than wait for the battle.

We got to John's house, which was close to the desert. The animals were with us every moment. We didn't want the enemy to know or feel anything until we got to the slope of the valley. There was no one outside the tents. They were all inside the tents.

Then we started the sweep. We attacked them in their tents. A large number of them surrendered, but some of them fought. William shot arrows and did not run out.

Finally, I saw Seymour. I wanted to see him in order to figure out his face. He was tall and had on a big hat. I saw him from afar. He didn't fight but escaped with the rest of his army. Beside him, I saw James, and behind him the cat I had talked to at the water source. She knew me and looked at me with surprise.

We put the captives in the middle. There was a lot of space in the tents—enough for us to walk in and look for prisoners inside the tents or loot anything we could benefit from. We covered the bodies of their dead.

There was a big tent at the end. I think it was the tent of their commander, Seymour. We made it the last thing we came to. I was the first to enter. I found a large munition that three or more people carry. I don't know why these munitions exist. I thought all along, *We had guns, and they didn't know about it.*

I found a round table in the middle of the tent. There were many yellow leaves, and there were some swords. I went to the yellow leaves, and I picked up a piece of paper and started reading the writing on it: "Dear sir: You must not hesitate in some of what we planned and progress in a timely manner when the alternative leader tells you to get ready. Get ready, and don't go out of obedience." I picked up another paper, and I read, "Nine o'clock."

The size of their army and their gear were greater than ours, but they were not perfect. We had taken them by surprise.

Some friends went to the water source. I stayed in the big tent with William, Leonard, David, and Linda. After about two hours, David said, "We should all go back now. We've been very fortunate in this victory. Everyone knows that they're bigger than us, and they've been superior to us for a long time."

Everyone came back to Frank's house, and as soon as we walked into his yard, Frank let us know that he was happy with our victory. He asked his bodyguards to bring all the city's people to his yard to celebrate this victory.

Frank began speaking to the people. He said, "Everyone should know that if Osemer hadn't told us about them a few hours before they attacked us, we wouldn't have won. We all learned today that weapons don't always mean power. Power is in the mind, if we can use it intelligently. I have a gift that I want to make to Osemer on this occasion for his efforts."

Sandy then came up behind me in the most beautiful clothes I'd ever seen her in.

Frank said, "The gift is Sandy. You will marry her, Osemer, and we will have a celebration on this day for two things: victory and Osemer marrying Sandy. My son, we will build for you a big castle to live in. You are now one of us."

Then I went up to the top of the house. I wanted to say something to them all. When I got to the podium, I started talking. "Listen to me, all of you. I'm very happy with this gift. My travels are going to end today. I will live among you. We were fortunate in this victory. Obviously, they have more than us in everything: weapons and gear and their huge numbers. Before we start the celebration, I want to say we should sit down a long time, plan, build, and use our brains to make things that the enemy cannot think of."

I told them, "Today we won by using our minds. We surprised them, and they didn't know we were coming. It was risky, but now we're going to build a little centre for crazy ideas. There's no idea too stupid. We'll be away from the fight for a long time so we can build, create, and innovate. I also want to rest in my house, which everyone will help me build. I want to take a long time off with my beautiful wife, Sandy, and maybe have some sons."

Frank said, laughing, "You heard what Osemer said. We should work on what he said. We will ambush anyone who tries to approach this city. I hope no one disturbs Osemer in his new home until he relaxes and takes the time he needs."

To Be Continued in Part 2

www.ingramcontent.com/pod-product-compliance
Ingram Content Group UK Ltd.
Pitfield, Milton Keynes, MK11 3LW, UK
UKHW041642190726
13854UKWH00006B/2648

9 781950 596782